Patient-Centric Communication

Skills for Healthcare Professionals

Table of Contents

Chapter 1. Introduction

In today's rapidly evolving healthcare landscape, a keystone factor that influences patient outcomes and satisfaction is the quality of communication. Welcome to our Special Report on "Patient-Centric Communication: Skills for Healthcare Professionals." We have meticulously prepared this report to spark your interest in exploring the art and science of empathetic interaction with patients. Far from being an austere, technical subject, our report is presented in an approachable yet comprehensive manner. You'll dive into fascinating case studies, practical strategies, and innovative models that will fortify the bond between healthcare practitioners and patients. This compelling journey is not a mere exposition but rather an experience designed to reshape your way of thinking about modern patient care. Whether you're a healthcare professional, a medical student, or simply a curious reader, this tailored report will feed your interest while equipping you with invaluable tools to enhance patient communication. So gear up to dive into an enriching exploration of patient-centric communication, one that's sure to amplify your knowledge and encourage you to better the world, one patient at a time.

Chapter 2. The Essence of Patient-Centric Communication

Patient-centric communication (PCC) isn't just a trendy jargon term in the healthcare field; it's the fundamental ethos of the patient care mission. As healthcare professionals, it is our responsibility to foster open, honest, and thoughtful dialogue with our patients, thereby enhancing patient satisfaction, improving health outcomes, and forging a stronger clinician-patient bond.

Primarily, PCC seeks to acknowledge the patient's experience, feelings, expectations, and socio-cultural background. Only when we wholly embrace the patient's perspective can we fully tune into their unique healthcare needs and craft bespoke strategies delivering optimal patient-guided care.

2.1. The Fundamentals of Patient-Centric Communication

Patient-centric communication is grounded in the principle of empathy. Empathy, in this context, is the willingness and ability to put oneself in the patient's shoes, understand their fears and concerns, and address them in a compassionate and informed manner.

A critical aspect of PCC is active listening. When patients feel heard and understood, their confidence in the healthcare provider rises, thereby enhancing adherence to prescribed therapies, better management of health conditions, and improved outcomes. Actively listening to a patient involves not only understanding what is being said but also perceived nonverbal cues.

Cultural competence also forms a bedrock of PCC. As healthcare providers, we serve people from diverse backgrounds and cultures, each bringing with them their own beliefs, practices, and expectations related to healthcare. Understanding and respecting these differences are vital to establishing trust and effective communication.

2.2. The Role of Nonverbal Communication in PCC

While verbal communication forms a significant part of patient interactions, nonverbal cues can tell a story on their own. Body language, facial expressions, posture, gestures, and tone of voice can often reveal unspoken thoughts and emotions. Reading and suitably responding to these nonverbal signals can greatly enhance the quality of clinician-patient interactions.

Patients often express their anxieties, fears, and concerns through non-verbal signals. Recognizing these cues can help us ease their worries, instill confidence, and improve their overall experience.

2.3. Barriers to Patient-Centric Communication

Despite its clear benefits, adoption of PCC is often hindered by several barriers, including time constraints, lack of training in communication skills, patient literacy levels, and engrained attitudes and behaviors. Educational initiatives focused on instilling empathetic listening and empathetic responding are crucial in addressing these barriers. By training clinicians to be not just healthcare providers but also empathetic communicators, we can pave the way for more holistic, patient-centered care.

Effective patient communication also means accommodating patients with limited health literacy or language proficiency. Simple solutions, such as avoiding medical jargon, using illustrations, or offering translation services, can significantly improve the clarity of communication.

2.4. The Influence of Technology on PCC

In today's digital age, technology is reshaping the ways in which we communicate with our patients. Telehealth services, patient portals, and mobile health applications are becoming increasingly prevalent. While these technologies can improve access to care, they also pose new challenges to maintaining patient-centered communication.

It's essential for healthcare professionals to adapt their communication styles to these new platforms, ensuring that they remain welcoming, respectful, and transparent in virtual interactions.

2.5. The Impact of PCC on Health Outcomes

Impressive evidence corroborates the fact that effective doctor-patient communication positively influences health outcomes. By developing partnerships with patients, providers can instill their trust, increase adherence to treatment regimens, and improve the perception of care. Additionally, numerous studies show that patient satisfaction directly correlates to their inclination to continue with treatment and follow-up.

2.6. Measuring Patient-Centric Communication

Quality measures for patient communication need to move beyond mere patient satisfaction scores. They should assess the communication skills of healthcare providers, capture the 'patient voice,' and evaluate whether patients feel respected, understood, and involved in their care decisions.

2.7. Practical Strategies for Enhancing PCC

Countless strategies exist to promote PCC. They include using open-ended questions, taking time to understand the patient's perception of their illness, expressing empathy, addressing patient concerns, confirming patient understanding, and discussing the next steps.

Ultimately, the provider's goal should be to make patients feel safe, heard, and valued. Such a conducive environment encourages patients to share information openly, promotes better informed decisions, and fosters strong patient-provider relationships.

By comprehensively understanding the essence, benefits, and challenges of patient-centric communication, healthcare professionals can significantly improve their interaction with patients. Through practice and reflection, we can create a healthcare system that truly respects and values the patient voice. In doing so, we will continue to evolve healthcare for the better – one conversation at a time.

Chapter 3. Recognizing and Bridging Cultural Gaps in Healthcare

Understanding cultural perspectives and acknowledging diversity are essential components of effective patient care. Healthcare providers who skillfully bridge cultural gaps can achieve better patient outcomes by maintaining a strong therapeutic alliance and enhancing patient satisfaction. This chapter will dismantle the complexities associated with cultural gaps in healthcare communication, highlighting strategies, case studies, and models tailored to improve communications, thereby consolidating more fruitful relationships between healthcare providers and their culturally diverse patients.

3.1. Why Cultural Sensitivity Matters

Cultural sensitivity in healthcare refers to being aware of, and appreciating, the different backgrounds, beliefs, and behaviors of patients. It recognizes that each individual's health beliefs, practices, and needs may be molded by a myriad of factors, including race, religion, ethnicity, socioeconomic status, language, age, sexual orientation, and disability status.

Cultural competency is more than just politeness or sensitivity; it's about understanding the patient's perspective. The effort made to understand the patient's cultural background can help create trust and establish a rapport, thereby enhancing the therapeutic alliance. A culturally sensitive healthcare provider can also gain crucial insights into a patient's health beliefs, practices, and experiences which may directly influence diagnosis, treatment, and follow-up care.

3.2. Cultural Competence and Its Relevance

Cultural competence refers to a set of congruent behaviors, attitudes, and policies that come together in a system, agency, or among health professionals to work effectively in cross-cultural situations. Pertinently, acknowledging cultural competence in healthcare can yield several significant benefits:

- Better understanding of health and belief systems, which can improve diagnosis and treatment.

- Enhanced patient-doctor relationships, leading to better communication and subsequently better adherence to prescribed treatments.

- Reduced health disparities owing to the ability to communicate effectively and understand the patient's health-related behaviors.

3.3. Building Cultural Competence

Cultural competence cannot be cultivated overnight. It is an enduring, evolving, dynamic process that necessitates a commitment to continuous learning, self-examination, and humility.

Here are some strategies that can help in establishing cultural competence:

- Cultivate curiosity: Develop an unquenchable thirst to learn about different cultures, traditions, and customs. Be non-judgmental and open to new experiences.

- Self-awareness: Reflect on your own cultural heritage, beliefs, biases, and prejudices. Recognize that your personal values might not universally apply.

- Training and education: Partake in workshops, seminars, courses, webinars, that focus on cultural competency in healthcare.

- Seek guidance: Discuss with colleagues or mentors from diverse cultural backgrounds for further comprehension.

3.4. Communication: The Key to Bridging Cultural Gaps

Effective communication sets the foundation for recognizing and bridging cultural gaps in healthcare settings. This section will delve into strategies to enhance communication skills:

- Learn and use key phrases in the patient's language: Even minimal efforts at using the patient's language can significantly impact trust-building.

- Use of professional interpreters: For patients with limited proficiency in the healthcare provider's language, use of professional interpreters can enhance the accuracy and completeness of communication.

- Nonverbal communication: Understand the cultural implications of bodily movements, gestures, eye contact, and spatial distances.

- Active Listening: Show genuine interest in what the patient is saying. Paraphrase, reflect, ask open-ended questions, and pay attention to the patient's non-verbal cues.

3.5. Case Studies in Cultural Competence

Several case studies elucidate the difference that culturally competent care can make to patient outcomes. One such case involved a Vietnamese woman admitted to the hospital for high fever and shortness of breath, who wasn't responding adequately to the antibiotics administered. After engaging an interpreter, the staff discovered that she was a devout Buddhist who was consuming only a vegetarian diet, which had not been recorded in her initial nutritional assessment. Adjusting her regimen to account for her diet and spiritual needs significantly improved her recovery.

It's also essential to learn from the lapses. A study published in the Journal of General Internal Medicine described a Japanese man who had an unsuccessful surgery due to culturally rooted communication barriers. Despite expressing doubts, the surgeon performed surgery owing to the patient's indirect agreement. Upon receiving a more culturally competent second opinion, the patient opted against surgery, demonstrating that cultural competence not only safeguards interests but can substantially reduce unnecessary patient care risks.

3.6. The Road Ahead

With ever-increasing cultural diversity, healthcare professionals must commit to lifelong learning wherein they continuously strive to improve their cultural competence. By recognizing the importance of cultural sensitivity and by adopting a culturally competent approach, they not only contribute to individual patient care but also aid in mitigating system-wide health disparities in multicultural societies. Armed with cultural competence and empathy, healthcare providers can reshape the trajectory of patient care one interaction at a time, one patient at a time.

Chapter 4. Building Trust: The Fundamentals of Empathy in Patient Interactions

Comprehensive patient care invariably embraces empathetic healthcare professionals who are able to build trust and strong relationships with their patients. Although medical knowledge and expertise are essential, they may not be sufficient. The distinct element that elevates care to the next level is empathy.

4.1. The Essence of Empathy

Plainly stated, empathy is the capacity to understand, experience and share another person's feelings. In the context of healthcare, it involves understanding a patient's experiences and emotions, and reliably transferring that understanding back to the patient. Empathy is demonstrated in patient interactions through three main elements: cognitive, emotional, and compassionate empathy.

Cognitive empathy, also known as perspective-taking, involves understanding the patient's feelings and thoughts without necessarily sharing them. Emotional empathy refers to the ability to share and respond to patients' emotions, and compassionate empathy goes a step further, compelling the healthcare professional to take action to alleviate the patient's suffering.

4.2. Role of Empathy in Building Trust

Trust forms the bedrock of the patient-healthcare provider relationship. Being empathetic can help the healthcare provider forge a close bond with the patient, encouraging open and candid communication. Patients who trust their providers are more likely to adhere to the prescribed treatment plan, show up for follow-up visits, and report better outcomes.

Empathy also impacts patient satisfaction. Patients with empathetic providers report higher levels of happiness with their care. Moreover, when patients feel understood and valued, they are more likely to engage in the shared decision-making process—an increasingly important aspect of modern healthcare.

4.3. The Art of Expressing Empathy

Expressing empathy is an art that can be learned and honed. One must first recognize the patient's emotion. This often relies on nonverbal cues. A frown, grimace, or the avoidance of eye contact can indicate pain, anxiety, or fear. Recognizing these cues will help the healthcare professional identify the patient's true feelings.

Once the emotion is identified, the healthcare professional should validate it. For example, saying, "I can see you're feeling anxious about the procedure," acknowledges the patient's feelings without any judgment.

Reflecting back the emotion is the next step. This can be done through statements like, "It sounds like this has been really challenging for you." Such responses show the patient that their feelings have been heard and understood.

Finally, the provider's reality should align with the patient's.

Reassuring the patient that their feelings are normal and understood can comfort them and make them feel less alone in their experience. Phrases like, "Many patients feel the same way before a procedure. It's completely normal to feel anxious," can help patients feel validated.

4.4. Communication Skills for Effective Empathy

To express empathy effectively, healthcare professionals should hone their communication skills. Active listening, for example, is a vital skill. This requires the provider to be fully present and engaged in the conversation, conveying interest and respect for the patient's point of view.

Paraphrasing and summarizing the patient's words also helps to demonstrate understanding. This can be done by restating the patient's words in a different or simpler way, or by summarizing the main points of the conversation.

Nonverbal communication also plays an important role in expressing empathy. Maintaining a relaxed posture, making appropriate eye contact, and using gentle, assuring touch can help the patient feel understood and comforted.

4.5. Measuring Empathy in Healthcare Providers

Measuring healthcare professionals' empathy levels is a growing trend in healthcare industry. Surveys such as the Jefferson Scale of Physician Empathy (JSPE) and the Consultation and Relational Empathy (CARE) measure can be used to analyze empathy levels.

These tools rely on a self-reported, questionnaire-based approach. As important as it is for these measures to be reliable, it is equally crucial for these measures to drive interventions aimed at improving empathy in the healthcare setting.

These efforts are not intended to create 'caring robots', but rather to help practitioners align their care more closely with their patients' needs and expectations.

4.6. Empathy Training: Cultivating the Skill

Commonly, empathy is considered innate, something you either do or do not possess. However, research suggests that empathy, much like a skill, can be developed with time and practice.

Various empathy training models exist, including cognitive-behavioral training, mindfulness-based approaches, and narrative medicine. These models aim to help healthcare professionals connect with their patients on a deeper level, understanding their experiences and emotions on a more authentic level.

Through continuous practice and training, healthcare professionals can learn to better recognize and respond to their patients' needs, improving patient care and satisfaction in the process.

In conclusion, empathy is an invaluable tool that can enhance patient trust, satisfaction, and outcomes. By understanding its importance, practicing empathetic communication skills and investing in empathy training, healthcare providers can create a more patient-centric approach to care, one which will surely benefit both patients and providers in the long run.

Hopefully, the narrative provided in this comprehensive report will serve as an insightful resource, enriching your understanding of empathy in healthcare, leading to improved patient communication and care.

Chapter 5. Communication Techniques for Difficult Conversations

In the realm of healthcare, technical expertise and medical knowledge contribute significantly to successful patient outcomes. However, mastery in communication, specifically during difficult conversations, often serves as the defining factor in achieving desirable results. This piece unravels the art of these challenging interactions, delving into numerous techniques, principles, and strategies. We have interspersed practical applications, case studies, and evidence-based research findings to make this guide as informative as possible.

5.1. Setting the Stage

Before directly engaging on clinical matters, it's necessary to tactfully set the stage for difficult conversations. Start by ensuring you have sufficient time for the discussion, with minimal interruptions. Make sure the setting is private and comfortable, reinforcing the patient's dignity during their vulnerable moments.

Establish the patient's understanding and expectation of the conversation. This clear communication prevents any false hope and maximizes patient understanding, reducing the likelihood of animosity or conflict. Additionally, involve family members or caregivers based on the patient's wishes and consent, as they can provide emotional support and aid in processing information.

5.2. Delivering Unfavorable News

Next, we navigate the tricky landscape of conveying unfavorable news. Break down the information into digestible parts using clear language, avoiding medical jargon whenever possible to avoid confusion. Start with a "warning shot," a statement that prepares the patient for the bad news. It can sound something like, "Unfortunately, I have some news that's not what we hoped for." Then, pause to allow the patient to mentally prepare for what's coming next.

Stepwise disclosure, revealing information gradually, can help protect the patient from being overwhelmed. Remember to summarize the information periodically and confirm their understanding before moving forward.

5.3. Dealing with Strong Reactions

Handling strong emotional reactions can be particularly challenging. The first step is to anticipate these emotional responses, which can range from disbelief, shock, anger, or grief. Allow the patient to express their feelings, and ensure your reactions show empathy and understanding. You might say, "I can see that this is really tough news for you. It's not what we had hoped for."

Avoid jumping immediately to silver linings or being overly optimistic. Instead, confirm their feelings, reassure them of your support, and give them the space to process their emotions.

5.4. Shared Decision Making

Embracing shared decision making is a key aspect of patient engagement in their health journey, especially when the path is riddled with challenging forks. This principle reinforces respect for patients' autonomy and fosters a stronger therapeutic relationship.

A patient's medical, emotional, and social needs vary, all influencing their treatment decisions. Being an active listener, acknowledging their concerns, and deliberating different options sincerely can empower patients in their healthcare journey.

Remember that patients may need time to absorb information, ask questions, and share their preferences. Involve family or caregivers, if appropriate, in these decisions to further support the patient.

5.5. Dealing with Conflict

Difficult conversations sometimes provoke conflicts, incongruent goals, or disagreements which can escalate emotions. Effective communication and negotiation skills are necessary tools in such situations.

Firstly, identify the root cause of the conflict, whether it be communication gaps, unmet expectations, or a divergence in medical goals. Use neutral, non-judgmental language, demonstrating respect for their feelings and perspectives. Instead of trying to prove your point, focus on establishing common ground and building consensus.

Adopting an assertive, rather than aggressive, style helps navigate conflict while preserving the integrity of the patient-provider relationship. This involves expressing your standpoint, feelings, or needs clearly and respectfully without infringing on the rights or beliefs of others.

5.6. Navigating End of Life Conversations

End of life conversations, generally deemed the most challenging, demand utmost sensitivity and skill. Key principles include truth-telling, empathy, encouraging questions, patient autonomy, and addressing fears and misconceptions surrounding death and dying.

Collaboratively discuss aspects like prognosis, expectations, do-not-resuscitate (DNR) orders, advanced care planning, palliative options, and spiritual or emotional topics. Ensure these discussions align with the patient's readiness, understanding, and cultural or personal beliefs. Strive to convey hope, not necessarily linked to cure, perhaps in improving quality of life, managing symptoms, or meeting their goals.

Though arduous and emotionally draining, successful difficult conversations can significantly enhance patient satisfaction, acceptance, and treatment adherence. Beyond techniques and strategies, remember that these conversations demand sincere empathy, attentiveness, and compassion to patient experiences and emotions. A true healer's art lies in skilfully mastering this balance.

Chapter 6. Digital Health: Technology's Role in Patient-Centric Communication

With rapid advancements in technology, the conventional patient-provider relationship in the healthcare setting is undergoing a holistic transformation. Digital health represents the convergence of health with digital and genomic technologies. It's an empowering tool that paves the way for patient-centric communication, allowing for the involvement of patients in the decision-making process regarding their health.

6.1. The Advent of Digital Health

In the 21st Century, with the proliferation of the Internet and smartphones, there was a significant rise in health-related internet use, thus giving birth to digital health. Technology entered the healthcare domain, creating a gateway for easier communication between patients and healthcare providers. Gone were the days of uninformed passivity as patients could now actively participate in their healthcare journey via technology's facilitation.

Digital health primarily includes health information technology (HIT), mobile health (mHealth), wearable devices, telehealth and telemedicine, personalized medicine, health information exchange (HIE), and the use of information and data to improve healthcare.

This section aims to articulate this state-of-the-art concept and its impact on how healthcare professionals communicate with patients. Understanding the nuances of digital health will equip us better to meet the demanding needs of the new-age patient.

6.2. Enabling Patient Engagement through Mobile Health (mHealth)

An important offspring of digital health is mobile health, or mHealth. It refers to the practice of using mobiles or wireless devices to support healthcare services. The use of mHealth applications has marked a considerable increase in patient engagement. It's because they put a wealth of information at the patient's fingertips, making the once layman an informed health consumer.

Applications facilitating symptom tracking, promoting medication adherence, providing remote monitoring, or even conducting an online consultation have become abundant. Patients are now more involved in their health decisions, thanks to these interactive and user-friendly platforms.

Studies underpin the effectiveness of mHealth applications in improving patient engagement, which, in turn, results in better health outcomes. For example, a study showed that medication adherence improved by 62% and asthma control by 80% when patients used a mobile application for monitoring. The introduction of digitally savvy patients has thus started setting the tone for a new level of interaction that healthcare providers have to adapt to.

6.3. Wearable Devices: The Silent Health Trackers

The advent of wearable devices such as fitness trackers and smart health devices has made health monitoring a continuous process. A pulse meter, glucose monitor, or sleep tracker – these devices are quietly revolutionizing healthcare by enabling accurate self-monitoring.

Wearable devices facilitate real-time tracking of health metrics, enabling patients to proactively manage their health. Patients can share this data with healthcare providers, paving the way for informed discussions and individualized health plans. These candid dialogues with healthcare providers about manageable behavior elements such as physical activity, diet, and sleep can play a crucial role in prevention and disease management.

6.4. Telehealth: Bridging the Gap

Telehealth brings healthcare to the patient's home, bridging the gap between people and healthcare systems. It allows for long-distance patient and clinician contact, care, advice, reminders, education, intervention, and remote admissions.

COVID-19 pandemic highlighted the significant role telehealth can play in maintaining the continuity of care and reducing exposure to disease. Consultations got streamlined through video calls, reducing the need for hospital visits and waiting times. It refocused communication between patients and healthcare providers, thus enabling active dialogue and clear conveyance of therapeutic strategies.

6.5. Health Information Exchange: Ensuring Continuity of Care

Health Information Exchange (HIE) involves the digital movement of health-related information among organizations per nationally recognized standards. By safely sharing patient data among healthcare providers, HIE ensures a seamless, coordinated, and comprehensive treatment experience for patients. It grants providers a holistic view of the patient's health status, facilitating informative discussions around care delivery.

6.6. Personalized Medicine: Tailoring Treatment for the Individual

Genomic technologies spur the development of personalized, or precision, medicine where treatments are tailored to individual patient's genetics. This means patients get treatments that are likely to help them based on genetic testing, which leads to better outcomes, fewer side effects, and cost-effective care.

Personalized medicine redefines the communication between healthcare practitioners and patients. It delves deep into understanding the individual's body, thereby facilitating an in-depth discussion around therapeutic implications and fostering a unique trust between the patient and the caregiver.

6.7. The Road Ahead: Future of Patient-Communication

Digital Health presents unprecedented opportunities to enhance patient-provider communication. However, a few challenges need tackling to fully utilize its potential. These challenges revolve around data privacy, patient data security, and healthcare professionals' digital literacy. Policies that strike a balance between tech-enhancement and the preservation of the traditional ethos of healing is crucial.

Moreover, technology should be viewed as an aid, not a replacement for the human touch that forms the foundation of caregiving. It is vital to remember that digital technology is just a tool. Ultimately, the cure lies in care.

Our exploration into digital health and the significant shift it brings into patient-centric communication paints a clear picture. Technology is transforming care, making it more personalized, immediate, and effective. The onus is on us, the healthcare providers, to find a balance, to marry the old with the new, to bring about the true digital health revolution. This fusion will pave the way for empathetic patient-centric healthcare communication that cherishes human values at its heart.

Chapter 7. Dealing with Patient Anxiety and Fear: A Human-Centered Approach

Beginning a conversation about patient anxiety and fear within the context of healthcare is tantamount to acknowledging the oft-ignored element of human-centered care. If we place a patient's emotional well-being under the spotlight, it unravels insights into their overarching health, recovery, and satisfaction. This chapter will delve into this perspective with a curious yet respectful mindset, exploring the tools and strategies healthcare professionals can employ to abate patient anxiety and fear.

7.1. Understanding Patient Anxiety and Fear

Before we delve into the strategies to address patient anxiety and fear, it's crucial to understand these emotional responses. Anxiety encompasses feelings of unease, such as worry or fear, and varies in severity, ranging from mild unease to debilitating panic attacks. On the other hand, fear is defined as an emotional response to a known or definite threat, triggering a fight-or-flight response.

More often than not, healthcare environments catalyze these conditions due to various factors, like the uncertainty of medical procedures, fear of diagnosis, discomfort due to physical symptoms, or even the impersonal nature of the clinical setting. A study by the Journal of Behavioural Medicine revealed that almost 25% of patients reported moderate to high levels of anxiety before routine check-ups. This statistic underscores the necessity for strategies to alleviate these negative emotional responses.

7.2. Tool 1: Empathy in Communication

Understanding a patient's perspective plays a pivotal role in calming their anxiety. Empathy, an ability that allows us to 'feel' from the patient's vantage point, is the cornerstone of this approach. It is the manifestation of the old adage, "put yourself in someone else's shoes." Expressing empathy begins with active listening. This entails not just hearing but also internalizing the patient's spoken and unspoken cues. The next step is validating their experiences - a simple acknowledgment can go a long way in establishing trust.

Orchestrating conversations that are conducive to sharing can also empower patients to voice their fears and anxieties. Open-ended, non-threatening questions like "How are you feeling about this?" can invite the patient to explore and express their emotions without fearing judgment.

7.3. Tool 2: Providing Clear Information

Fear and anxiety often stem from the unknown or misunderstood elements of a healthcare scenario. Dispelling uncertainties through clear, straightforward communication of medical procedures, potential results, and care plans can significantly alleviate patient anxiety. A recent study in the British Journal of Anaesthesia found that thorough preoperative information reduces anxiety in patients.

However, providing information does not equate to bombarding patients with medical jargon - rather, the communication must be streamlined to suit the patient's comprehension level. Using visual aids and simple analogies can simplify complex information and fortify the patient's understanding.

7.4. Tool 3: Fostering a Comforting Environment

Stark white walls and the cold, clinical ambience of healthcare settings subtly fuel patient anxiety. By fine-tuning these environmental factors, healthcare professionals can create a safe, comforting environment fostering tranquillity. Soft, calming colors on the walls, ambient music, and access to natural light can form part of an anxiety-reducing setup. A study made by the National Center for Biotechnology Information demonstrates how access to natural views can reduce patient stress and improve satisfaction rates.

Beyond the physical environment, humanizing interactions contribute to this comforting atmosphere. A warm introduction, maintaining non-verbal communication like eye-contact, and presenting a friendly demeanor can act as assured signs of care and safety for the patient.

7.5. Tool 4: Guided imagery and relaxation techniques

When patients are left alone with their thoughts, anxiety tends to escalate. Guided imagery and relaxation techniques function as psychological tools to combat this spiralling effect. Guided imagery involves the use of calming, pleasant scenes, which the patient visualizes. Healthcare professionals can guide patients along this visualization, leading to relaxation and distraction from the stress-inducing stimuli.

Relaxation techniques, such as mindful breathing and progressive muscle relaxation, can also help patients regain control over their bodily reactions to anxiety and fear. These techniques can be taught to patients, empowering them to manage their reactions even in the absence of a healthcare professional.

7.6. Tool 5: Incorporating Predictable Routines

Uncertain scenarios are potent triggers for anxiety and fear. Predictable routines help to counter this by allowing patients to anticipate the sequence of events. This understanding helps to reinstall a sense of control, thus naturally reducing the intensity of their anxiety. These routines can include a consistent daily schedule, standardised information delivery, and even regular staff rotations.

In conclusion, dealing with patient anxiety and fear requires an integrated, human-centered approach. It's about acknowledging the human beneath the hospital gown, their emotions, and fears. With a toolbox ranging from empathetic communication and clear information to guided relaxation techniques, healthcare professionals can aid in alleviating anxiety, promoting a more patient-centric and emotionally considerate healthcare experience. It's not merely a strategy, but a paradigm shift towards more compassionate, holistic care that reverberates on both patients' satisfaction and their health outcomes.

Chapter 8. Empowering Patients through Clear Communication

The evolving dynamics of the healthcare industry require a renewed focus on patient-centric communication. Clear and effective communication encourages patients to participate actively in their care, leading to improved treatment outcomes and increased patient satisfaction. This chapter delves deep into the concept of empowering patients through clear communication, outlining strategies for healthcare professionals to adopt and integrate into their practice.

8.1. Engaging Patients: The First Step

Engagement forms the bedrock of patient empowerment. A healthcare professional's ability to engage their patients in a meaningful dialogue opens the channels for clear and effective communication. Narrative medicine, which values the patient's own recounting of their story, provides the foundation for this engagement. Creating a safe and empathetic space for patients to share their experiences and concerns allows them to feel heard and acknowledged, fostering a sense of trust and setting the stage for proactive involvement in their care.

8.2. The Science and Art of Listening

Effective communication hinges on good listening skills. Active listening, a technique that involves giving undivided attention to the speaker, reflecting, and providing affirmative responses, demonstrates respect for the patient's perspective and fosters a mutual understanding. It encourages patients to share crucial information about their symptoms, health history, and lifestyle, which directly impact their overall treatment plan. In addition to the dissemination of important medical knowledge, active listening also empowers patients by acknowledging their fears and anxieties.

8.3. Communication Tailored to Individual Needs

Understanding a patient's psychosocial context – their lifestyle, cultural background, social circumstances and mental health – is key to tailoring communication to individual needs. Customising medical advice and guidance according to a patient's unique situation fosters better understanding, acceptance, and compliance with the prescribed treatment. Incorporating personalized communication strategies not only improves patient adherence but also enhances the therapeutic alliance.

8.4. Harnessing the Power of Non-Verbal Communication

Non-verbal communication, comprising facial expressions, tone of voice, body language, and eye contact, plays an invaluable role in establishing a connection with patients. Positive non-verbal cues like maintaining eye contact and a calm tone of voice signal empathy, respect, and attentiveness. In contrast, negative non-verbal cues can often erode trust and hinder clear communication. Healthcare professionals must understand the significance of non-verbal cues to build rapport and improve patient interaction.

8.5. Implementing Teach-Back Method for Patient Education

Health literacy is a critical factor influencing patient empowerment. The teach-back method – asking patients to repeat back the given information or instruction in their own words – is an effective tool to assess their understanding and recall of crucial healthcare information. This technique encourages patient participation, enhances retention of information, and provides an opportunity to clear any misconceptions, thereby ensuring that patients are equipped to make informed decisions about their care.

8.6. Embracing Technology for Improved Communication

With the advent of digital health technologies, the healthcare communication landscape has undergone a significant transformation. Patient portals, telemedicine services, and mobile health applications facilitate easy access to healthcare resources and improved communication. These tools serve as an additional platform for clear communication between healthcare providers and patients, fostering accessibility, convenience, and continuity of care.

This exhaustive examination of clear communication's role in patient empowerment shapes a pathway towards a more patient-centric healthcare future. By adopting these strategies, healthcare professionals can facilitate patient empowerment, fostering improved health outcomes, patient satisfaction, and superior healthcare delivery.

Chapter 9. The Role of Non-Verbal Communication in Patient Care

Non-verbal communication plays a critical role in the patient-caregiver relationship. It acts as an invisible thread of connectivity that can shape treatment outcomes, enhance patient satisfaction, and promote therapeutic patient relationships. In the tapestry of effective healthcare delivery, non-verbal cues are interwoven with verbal dialogue, silently emanating messages that can build trust, show empathy, and create comfort.

9.1. Anatomy of Non-Verbal Communication

Non-verbal communication is a broad umbrella, covering a spectrum of silent behaviors and signals that convey intent, emotions, and perceptions. There are several essential types of non-verbal communication in healthcare. These include facial expressions, body language and posture, gestures, physical touch, space proximity, and even factors like room ambiance and attire.

Facial expressions often reveal emotions that words may not fully express. A warm smile can reassure an anxious patient, while an attentive, caring gaze can make a patient feel understood. Similarly, body language contributes significantly to non-verbal communication. An open posture can indicate an attitude of acceptance and readiness to help, while closed arms may send the message of disinterest or aloofness.

Gesture, another important aspect, can hinder or enhance communication. Positive gestures such as nodding show agreement and attentiveness, whereas negative gestures might include abrupt movements or pointing fingers, which can seem confrontational or intimidating.

Touch, when used appropriately, is a powerful tool. It can demonstrate professional confidence and empathy towards a patient. In contrast, the lack of it can be equally impactful, creating distance and impersonal relationships.

Lastly, space and ambiance act as silent, continuous signals. A clean, comforting environment not only encourages a sense of safety but also sends a message about the caregiver's ability and competence.

9.2. The Power of Silent Advocacy

Studies have shown that in many cases, non-verbal communication surpasses verbal exchanges in conveying empathy, understanding, and compassion. These silent signals can bridge cultural or linguistic gaps and can dissolve the walls of discomfort or apprehension. Especially in healthcare, where patients often deal with fear and vulnerability, it becomes essential for caregivers to master these non-verbal skills.

Patients interpret non-verbal cues, consciously or subconsciously, and these interpretations can affect their attitudes towards treatment. For example, a surgeon's firm handshake coupled with a confident smile could instill faith in a worried patient about to undergo surgery.

9.3. Evidence-Based Impact of Non-Verbal Communication

Interestingly, a lot of scientific research has emphasized the impact of non-verbal cues in patient-care. Various studies have drawn a connection between a practitioner's non-verbal behavior and the patient's adherence to medication, perception of care, and overall satisfaction.

A study published in the Journal of Nonverbal Behavior, observed that in patient-physician interaction, non-verbal communication had a greater influence on patient satisfaction than verbal communication did. High-quality non-verbal behavior was linked with reduced patient distress and increased satisfaction in another research conducted by the American Academy of Family Physicians. Thus, the evidence supporting the immense power of non-verbal cues in healthcare is compelling.

Furthermore, these cues can also help decipher a patient's state of mind and feelings. Patients who exhibit certain non-verbal cues may be feeling stress, fear, anxiety, or are withholding information. Recognizing these signs can provide an added layer for diagnosis or pave the path for important conversations.

9.4. Nurturing Non-Verbal Skills in Healthcare

Considering the immense importance of non-verbal communication, an intentional effort to nurture such skills among healthcare professionals has become a rising need. This need is also being championed by global bodies like the World Health Organization, underlining its role in patient-centered care, a cornerstone to the delivery of quality health services.

Healthcare training programs may feature educational modules on non-verbal communication, providing hands-on experience via role plays, case studies, and simulations. Many institutions also provide advanced training to help professionals recognize subtle patient cues, manage non-verbal contradictions (e.g., when verbal and non-verbal cues conflict), and practice controlled, self-aware communication.

Moreover, organizations can foster an environment that empowers non-verbal communication by arranging networking opportunities and forums where medical practitioners can share and learn from real-life scenarios, anecdotal experiences, and best practices.

9.5. Reflection and Conclusion

Non-verbal communication, while often overshadowed, is a potent skill in healthcare. Its role in patient care is multifaceted, influencing not only the therapeutic relationship but also impacting treatment adherence, satisfaction, and overall happiness of patients. By harnessing non-verbal cues appropriately, healthcare practitioners can deliver optimal care, enhancing patient satisfaction and outcomes. Going forward, medical curriculums and professional training modules should aim to enhance these essential skills to ensure meaningful and well-rounded patient care.

Chapter 10. Patient Education: Strategies for Explaining Complex Health Topics

For many healthcare professionals, simplifying and communicating complex health issues is often a challenging task. A patient's understanding is foundational in their ability to navigate the labyrinth of healthcare decisions capably. Accordingly, adopting effective strategies to clarify complex topics is indispensable.

10.1. The Art of Simplifying Complex Information

Mastering the art of distilling complex health information into comprehensible nuggets is a pivotal aspect to patient education. One way to achieve this is through the technique known as the universal precaution approach. Developed with the intent to clarify complicated health topics, it involves simplifying information regardless of the patients' perceived literacy skills.

Opting for plain language is an effective way to simplify complex subjects. It involves avoiding medical jargon and replacing them with everyday words. For instance, a term like 'hypertension' can be translated into 'high blood pressure.' Explaining concepts in a patient-friendly manner can truly bridge the communication gap and promote better understanding.

Creating analogies can also be beneficial in communicating complex health topics. Drawing parallels between medical conditions and daily life situations can help patients quickly conceptualize their conditions. Analogies offer a visual or relatable context, making information more digestible and easier to remember.

10.2. Crafting Clear Written Materials

Ensuring enhanced clarity in written patient materials is just as significant as oral communication. Use friendly, conversational working and break complicated information down into smaller, understandable segments. Offer summaries or take-home points for patients to review at their leisure, further embedding their understanding.

Use of images and infographics is another potent tool to simplify complex topics. Visuals activate different cognitive processes than text, which can be advantageous when explaining complex health conditions or procedures. Involve a designer for producing high-quality, clean, and engaging visual materials to supplement your written information.

10.3. Use of Digital Tools in Patient Education

Digital health tools can be harnessed to facilitate patient education. These technologies can offer interactive learning experiences, personalization, and provide a dynamic platform for healthcare professionals to delve into complex health topics.

Health apps could be a convenient path to deliver health education. They offer an interactive platform and can access various resources such as videos, interactive games, quizzes, and infographics. Mobile apps can also provide personalised information based on a patient's condition, age, literacy level, and other factors.

Virtual Reality (VR) offers another innovative platform for health education. Highly immersive, VR can simulate medical conditions or procedures with a high degree of realism allowing patients to fully understand their health predicaments.

10.4. Encouraging Active Patient Participation

Active patient participation is crucial in their education. To encourage this, try to foster a supportive environment that welcomes questions and feedback from the patient. They should feel comfortable expressing any confusion or concerns they have regarding their health.

Emphasize the use of Teach-back method, where patients get to explain or demonstrate the information they received. This reinforces the learning process and is a surefire way to gauge whether they fully comprehend the information provided.

10.5. Building Health Literacy

Helping patients build health literacy skills is fundamental in their ability to understand complex health topics. Providers can offer resources and tools to help patients build their health literacy skills, enabling them to understand health materials better and ask insightful questions about their conditions.

Remember, a patient's understanding of their health condition directly influences their ability to comply with treatment, manage their symptoms, and maintain their wellbeing. Learning to convey complex health topics in digestible, meaningful ways will enable healthcare professionals to better serve their patients, thus improving their outcomes and quality of life.

Chapter 11. Future of Patient-Centric Communication: Trends and Predictions

There's an adage that the only constant is change, and nowhere does this ring truer than in the world of healthcare. The future of patient-centric communication draws upon cutting-edge strategies, integrated technologies, and innovative tools. In this chapter, we'll delve into in-depth exploration of the future trends and predictions, including new methodologies, the role of technology, the importance of empathy, and regulator policies' potential impact.

11.1. Trends Emerging in Patient-Centric Communication

As more healthcare organizations align their efforts toward a patient-centered approach, trends and practices unique to patient-centric communication have emerged.

The era of One-Size-Fits-All communication is gradually fading away, replaced by tailored interactions catering to the patients. Personalized care maps are being created, considering individual lifestyles, health patterns, ethnic, cultural, language, and communication preferences, and others.

Another vital trend is the increasing emphasis on empathy-led communication. Doctors are no more seen merely as 'disease-curing' entities but more like 'health-coaching' allies. Acknowledging patients' concerns, fears, and anxieties, and providing advice with empathy, is being recognized as the way forward.

Additionally, shared decision-making is becoming the norm. This approach embraces a collaborative model where healthcare professionals and patients share equal responsibility, discuss options and potential outcomes, and agree on a common path.

11.2. The Role of Technology

How are digital health technologies shaping the patient-centric communication space? The answer is - in exceptional ways.

Telemedicine is on the rise, enabling patients and healthcare professionals to connect virtually, reducing the need for physical proximity. It is beneficial for routine check-ups, chronic disease management, and follow-up consultations.

Healthcare Chatbots and digital assistants are becoming regular companions for patients, providing information, offering reminders, and facilitating appointments. These AI-powered tools can provide personalized advice by analyzing patient data.

Moreover, Electronic Health Record (EHR) integration helps provide a consolidated view of the patient's medical history, thus aiding in informed decision-making.

Wearable health equipment and IoT in healthcare are no more a figment of one's imagination. They provide real-time, actionable health data, enabling timely interventions, and shaping a proactive health management regime.

11.3. Empathy in the Digital Age

In the digital healthcare scenario, cultivating empathy might seem challenging. The key resides in the balance - in combining digital convenience with the human touch.

It includes clear, empathetic language in digital interactions, 'human-like' dialogues with AI assistants, or in personalized video consultations. Even the written communication in a patient portal or an app exchange should echo empathy, understanding, and compassion.

11.4. Regulatory Policies shaping the Confluence of Healthcare and Technology

Regulatory policies have a significant role in shaping how technology integrates into healthcare and subsequently influences patient-centric communication.

Policies oriented towards data security and privacy safeguards are critical. Clarity in norms around telemedicine services across state and national boundaries, rules around health insurance portability, and mandates around EHR are some regulatory areas that have the potential to either facilitate or hinder the growth of patient-centric communication.

Similarly, standards prescribed for health-related apps and digital tools affect their acceptance and usage.

11.5. The Future... a Prediction

Looking ahead, we predict that the future will present an even more integrated and cohesive system where healthcare professionals, patients, their caregivers, and the entire healthcare ecosystem communicate seamlessly. The ultimate goal is to align healthcare delivery with patients' needs, values, and preferences, thereby improving the quality of care, enhancing health outcomes, and elevating patient satisfaction.

Influence of AI and machine learning will grow phenomenally, personalizing and democratizing health information like never before.

Finally, the increasing emphasis on teaching communication skills in medical curricula indicates that future generations of healthcare professionals will be equipped, not just medically, but also emotionally to cater to their patients.

There's a long journey ahead, but with patient-centric communication at the helm, the voyage is bound to be an enlightened one. This is not the end of the narrative – far from it. It's merely a stepping stone towards a future where healthcare communication does more than cure diseases; it transforms lives.